BIG DATA FOR BUSINESS

THE COMPLETE GUIDE TO UNDERSTAND

DATA SCIENCE, DATA ANALYTICS AND

DATA MINING TO BOOST MORE GROWTH

AND IMPROVE BUSINESS

Also by Victor Finch

wwwwwwww

Data Analytics For Beginners: Your Ultimate Guide To Learn and Master Data Analytics. Get Your Business Intelligence Right – Accelerate Growth and Close More Sales

See more books: https://www.auvapress.com/books

Leave a review on Amazon:

https://www.auvapress.com/amazon-review/big-data-business

THE COMPLETE GUIDE

BIG DATA

TO UNDERSTAND DATA SCIENCE, DATA ANALYTICS AND DATA MINING

FOR BUSINESS

TO BOOST MORE GROWTH AND IMPROVE BUSINESS

VICTOR FINCH

AUVA PRESS

Trademarks:

Auva Press and the Auva Press logo are trademarks or registered trademarks and may not be used without written permission. All other trademarks are the property of their respective owners and use in an editorial fashion to the benefit of the trademark owner, with no intention of infringement of the trademark.

FIRST EDITION

ISBN-13: 978-1-9739-5766-9
ISBN-10: 1-9739-5766-3

Editor: Amy James
Cover Designer: Howard West

To my loved ones and friends, friendship and to my family,
who make my world more purposeful and meaningful

CONTENTS

PREFACE

We are living in a world driven by and loaded with data. Today, data is revolutionizing firms in ways we would have never imagined decades ago. So much data—what is commonly called big data—of what we do is either being recorded or stored somewhere. Firms, both big and small, traditional or non-traditional, are using big data to understand their customers better.

As a matter of fact, big data helps target the appropriate customers and improve their purchasing experiences. The insights gained from analyzing big data helps firms to identify new growth areas and product opportunities, streamline their costs, increase their operating margins, and above all, make better human resource decisions and more efficient budgets.

Big data is impacting our world and for that matter, our lives. It impacts everything from the healthcare sector to the sporting industry. The list is endless. In fact, big data has already started a journey that will only expand at exponential rates for the next couple of decades.

By 2020, data scientists have predicted that there will be a massive 4300 percent increase in annual data generated by individuals and companies.

If you're thinking of a career in big data, then this book will open your eyes to that world. Every big data related role will create employment opportunities for the majority of experts outside of the IT sphere, so landing that dream job in big data won't be a problem.

Because big data analytics will drive every facet of our world, the success of any organization depends on how effective and aggressive the company uses big data analytics. Unfortunately, despite all the hype created around big data and analytics,
many people and organizations still don't understand these data-related buzzwords.

That is why you should consider exploring this book. The book aims to provide you with a sound understanding of big data and analytics, modern tools and technologies used in big data and the applications of big data in industries and businesses.

Welcome.

Chapter 1

Synopsis of Analytics

Before we discuss the world of big data and analytics, we must first understand the foundation of analytics. Understanding the basics of analytics will help you get a complete big picture view of big data analytics. So let's dive in.

Let's begin by answering a fundamental question: What is analytics?

What is analytics?

Analytics can range from any simple exploration to how well a specific product made last year sold, to a complex neural network model that predicts which clients to target for next year's marketing campaign. Such a process must entail extensive use of data by performing the statistical and quantitative analysis.

The aim of analytics is to explore the data using either exploratory of predictive models and make fact-based information in management to drive decision and actions.

Plainly speaking, analytics can be regarded as the analysis of data to extract hidden insights that will aid in decision-making.

Look around you.

Analytics is everywhere. Analytics is an integral component at most firms. But you don't need to be a data scientist to do the analysis. Analytics is a fundamental skill that you should have to run any business successfully.

Conventional applications of analytics require and eye for predicting future business performances and the ability to enhance them.

One must study business data using statistical analysis tools to uncover and understand any historical patterns.

For instance, a call center manager can analyze his team's performance data to optimize his/her human resource team. HR managers use their employee data to predict the rates of retention.

If you are a marketer, you can use your sales and marketing ROI to make optimal decisions for allocation of the marketing budget.

The bottom line is every firm is leveraging big data and analytics in one way or another to extract hidden insights. These days, firms are generating large amounts of data files.

These files are created from multiple sources and can exist in different locations across the organization's data storage infrastructure.

In some cases, the files may contain structured data, which can be easily manipulated using RDBMSs such as SQL Server, MySQL.

However, for the majority of cases, the files will include unstructured and semi-structured data that is presented in the form of documents, emails and other types of digital media.

Unlike the structured data, which can be easily manipulated by the standard RDBMS's, both semi-structured and unstructured data—or big data for that matter—are difficult to process using the standard RDBMS's.

The volume of big data created by the company can not only put so much strain on its storage resources but also strain on its processing capabilities.

From the storage resource perspective, handling any big data in the company means locating and removing the files that are obsolete, duplicated, or are non-essential in the organization.

Consequently, it will take a lot of time and energy to search through each of the storage files for data that should be archived or even deleted.

If you fail to archive and delete these files, they will continue to consume your valuable and limited hard disk storage capacity.

What about the processing capabilities?

From the resource- processing perspective, manipulating big data requires applying appropriate statistical methods and techniques that can help unearth insightful fact-based information that will aid in decision-making.

With the use of proper statistical and computing skills, you can quickly assess the current state of big data and take actionable steps to retrieve any valuable information while mitigating the risk of compliance-related challenges.

Here are some reasons why you should consider investing in data analytics:

- You'll establish a dialogue with your consumers. Today's customers are tough to understand. Data analytics can allow you to profile clients for a proper understanding of their needs.

- You'll re-examine your products and improve. Data analytics will provide invaluable insight into customer perceptions of your product. These sentiments can help you segment your market based on geographical or time zone requirements.

- You'll be in a position to perform risk analysis with your data. Predictive analysis of your data will enable your firm to gather data for helpful insight that keeps you updated about business environments.

- You'll now generate new revenue streams. You can sell any patterns you obtain from your data to non-personalized large firms and expand your revenue base.

Descriptive vs. Predictive Analytics

There are two types of analytics

- Descriptive analytics
- Predictive analytics

While descriptive analytics describes what has happened in the past, predictive analytics predicts what will occur in the future.

For instance, you have a sales report of a company, like Coca-Cola, for example. This report can tell you how many units of Coca-Cola were sold, where they were sold, at what price and a lot of other things.

All of this is information that will be emanating from the data. At this stage, all you are doing is simply slicing and dicing your data in different ways, looking at it from different perspectives, and along different dimensions.

There is minimal use of statistics in descriptive analytics, and so you don't have to master statistical techniques to be a data scientist for descriptive analytics.

While the descriptive analytics is a potent analytical tool, it will still gives you information about the past. But a business owner's primary concern is always the future. If you run a hotel, you want to be in a position to predict how many of your rooms will be occupied next month.

If you have a drug company, you want to know for a fact how which of your under-tested experimental drugs will most likely succeed.

This is where the predictive analytics comes in.

Predictive analytics works by identifying the patterns in historical data and then using statistical techniques to make inferences about the future.

At a very simplistic level, you'll try to fit the data into a specified pattern, and if you believe that the data is following a certain pattern, then you can predict what is going to happen in the future.

Let's examine a couple of small examples to elucidate this point better. Let's consider a retail business. Retailers are interested in understanding relationships between their products.

In particular, they want to know if a buyer selects product A, what is the probability that he/she will buy another product, B or C?

We call this product affinity analysis, association analysis or market basket analysis (MBA). MBA is commonly used in the retail businesses.

Suppose you're selling fruits. Buyers usually buy fruits in groups. That is, if a customer is purchasing one type of fruit, then he/she is likely to buy other kinds as well.

Therefore, it makes sense to always package all the fruits together in one place in the store.

If you're selling bread, then you should place the bread next to the peanut butter. Obviously, many of these relationships are fairly instinctual, but once in a while, you'll come across associations that are less obvious, which you wouldn't have discovered without the data analysis.

Let's consider another industry—Telecom firms.

Customer attrition rate is the rate at which customers leave the telecom company's services for another competitor's services.

This is a very common and important occurrence in the Telecoms industries. Most of us as consumer are guilty of such activity. The Telecom firms would love to predict which of their clients are likely to leave their service in the future.

Predictive modeling can enable them to predict which the type of customers is more likely to switch to another service.

For instance, if a customer's telephone usage has gone down drastically in the last couple of months, this could be an indicator that they are more likely to attrite.

But this is just one factor that we have identified in the Telecom industry. In reality, the combination of these elements usually acts as a more effective indicator.

Ideally, prescriptive analytics will go beyond the predictive analytics by not only predicting what is going to happen but also will also suggest the most optimal decisions that could happen under different scenarios.

It can include concepts such as optimization and simulation.

Conventional Analytical Tools

By now, you're probably wondering, "Which analytical tools can I use with my data?"

The analytical tools that you can use today with your data can be grouped into categories:

- Closed source/proprietary analytical tools

- Open source analytical tools

Let's jump in and explore these tools.

Closed source/proprietary tools

These are applications that are commercial in nature. In other words, you must purchase them before you begin to use them.

Obviously, their source codes—instructions written in a particular programming language—for these applications belong to their software developer, and the app can only be used as it is without modifications.

Examples of closed source apps for performing analytics are:

#1: SAS

SAS is an application that can mine, modify, manage and extract data from a variety of sources and perform statistical analysis on it.

The SAS app provides a graphical user interface for the non-technical users and has more advanced options that are provided through the SAS programming language.

17

The SAS programs have a DATA step that retrieves and process data creating an SAS data set, and the PROC step that analyzes the data.

#2: WPS

The WPS system can use programs written in SAS without the need for converting them into any other language.

WPS is compatible with the SAS applications. It is sometimes used as an alternative to SAS because it is relatively cheaper.

#3: MS Excel

Ms Excel is a spreadsheet software developed by Microsoft for Microsoft Windows and Mac OS. It has the following features: calculation, graphing, pivot tables, and a macro programming language (Visual Basic for Applications).

Most of the functional specific skills such as data mining, visualization, and statistical applications are provided in MS Excel.

You can begin by learning the fundamental concepts such as the workbook, worksheets, formula bar, and the ribbon.

#4: Tableau Software

Tableau Software is an American computer software company that is headquartered in Seattle. It develops a family of interactive data visualization products that are focused on business intelligence.

It has five main products: Tableau Desktop, Tableau Server, Tableau Online, Tableau Reader and Tableau Public that you can use for data analysis.

#5: Pentaho

Pentaho is a company that develops Pentaho Business Analytics, a software that applies Business Intelligence (BI) to provide data integration, OLAP services, data mining, reporting, dashboarding and ETL.

#6: Statistica

Statistica is a statistics and analytics software tool developed by StatSoft.

It offers data analysis, data management, data mining, statistics, and data visualization tools that you can use for analytics.

#7: Qlikview

Qlikview is a BI software from the Qlik Company. It helps its end users understand the business in a better way by providing them with features such as consolidating relevant data from multiple sources, exploring the different types associations in the data and enabling social decision making through their secure and real-time collaboration.

#8: MATLAB

MATLAB is a high-performance language that is meant for technical computing. It easily integrates the computation, visualization, and programming in an environment where problems and solutions can be expressed in a conversant programming notation.

MATLAB allows data scientists to solve many technical computing problems, especially those that can be modeled in in matrix and vector formats in:

- Data exploration, analysis, and visualization

- Mathematics and computation
- Development of algorithms
- Modeling, prototyping, and simulations
- Scientific and engineering graphics

Open source analytic tools

The second category of analytic tools is the so-called open source tools. By open source, it means you can access them freely and begin to use them. Also, their source code is open.

This means you can modify it to suit your needs. Here are examples of open source analytical tools:

#1: R programming

R is very useful for data analytics due to its versatile nature especially in the field of statistics. It is an open source software that provides data scientists with a variety of features for analyzing data.

Here are reasons that make R popular in data analytics:

- It is simple, well developed and one of the dynamic programming languages that support loops recursive functions, conditionals, and input/output facilities.

- It provides programming operators that can perform calculations on vectors, arrays, matrices, and lists.
- It has storage facilities, so data analysts can efficiently handle their data.
- It has graphical services that data analysts can use to display processed data.

#2: Python programming

Python is a potent, open source and flexible programming language that is easy to learn, use and has powerful libraries for data manipulation, management, and analysis.

Its simple syntax is easy to learn and resembles MatLab, C or C++ or Java. If you have core competencies in these programming languages, you'll not have a problem with Python language.

#3: Perl

Perl is a dynamic and high-level programming language that you can use for data analytics. Originally developed as a scripting language for UNIX by Larry Wall, Perl has provided its UNIX-like features and flexibility of any programming language to develop robust and scalable systems.

#4: Google Analytics

It is a service that creates detailed statistics about a website's traffic and the traffic sources. It also measures lead conversion rates and sales.

The product is developed for marketers to understand the website's performance regarding lead generation.

#5: Spotfire

The TIBCO Spotfire is an analytics and BI platform that analyzes data using predictive and complex statistical techniques.

There you have it—all the fundamentals of analytics. Obviously, the topic is inconclusive. There is a lot that takes place in the world of analytics!

Fortunately, you can grab my prequel book, *Data Analytics: Your Ultimate Guide for Beginners* to explore all the basics of analytics.

Specifically, you'll learn about the following:

- Basics of data analytics
- Descriptive statistics
- Visualization of data in Ms Excel
- Applications of analytics in industries

Chapter 2

Introduction to Big Data

Over-reliance on Data-driven and fact-based decision making will continue to grow. Today, we are witnessing widespread usage of metrics and reports where companies are using predictive analytics insights as part of their regular dashboards.

All the Data-driven and fact-based decisions today are based on big data.

But what is big data? And more specifically, how is big data and analytics correlated?

How is big data being used in organizations?

This chapter introduces you to the ins and outs of big data, so that you have a complete picture view of its applications in businesses and industries.

Let's dive in.

What is big data?

As a result of fast-paced, ever-evolving and complex technologies, new devices and communication channels such as social media platforms that we are witnessing, the volume of data being produced is increasing every year.

By 2020, data scientists have predicted that there will be a massive 4300 percent increase in annual data generated by individuals and companies.

 Consider this data sample.

The amount of data produced by individuals and companies from the beginning of time until 2003 were only 5 Billion GB!

Today, that figure has climbed sharply to slightly over 8.8 ZettaBytes! By 2020, this number will be hovering around 44 ZettaBytes. Even though this data being generated is meaningful and can unearth vital and insightful information for businesses, it is still being neglected.

This is what forms the big data.

It is a collection of large datasets, which can't be processed using conventional computing technologies such as RDBMS.

While the normal data is structured (and therefore, it can easily be processed using conventional technologies such as RDBMS), big data is semi-structured.

It includes files such as XML files and in extreme instances unstructured files such as data from Word, PDF, or other text files.

Big data can be characterized by the following:

- **Volume.** Big data is voluminous. And its volume just keeps on expanding over time!
- **Velocity.** Big data is generated at an exponential rate!

- **Variety.** Data will come in from all sorts of formats beginning from structured and numerical data in traditional databases to unstructured text documents, emails, PDFs, videos, and financial transactions.

Because of the above properties of big data, a lot of resource strain—from both the storage and processing capabilities—will be placed on the organization.

From the storage capacities point of view, organization will need to plan in advance for growing voluminous set of data and managing these data in a smart way that does no compromise the integrity of these data and balancing the limited disk space.

Data management is as important as data processing.

With proper data management plan in place, lots of time, money and energy can be saved during retrieval of data files. Resources can put to better use and channel into other data work.

From the processing capabilities, you don't just want to find out how much data you're storing but rather what can you do with that data?

You want to process the data to find out some answers that can help your organization compete favorably in these complex and ever-changing business environments.

Manipulating such data requires the application of appropriate statistical methods and techniques that can contribute to unearthing insightful fact-based information for decision making.

With the use of proper statistical and computing skills, you can easily assess the current state of big data and take actionable steps to retrieve any valuable information while mitigating the risk of compliance-related challenges.

Why big data analytics?

To understand the importance of big data in today's business environment, let me use an example of a company that I will simply refer to as XYZ.

XYZ is a retail chain that sells equipment for adventure sporting activities such as trekking, climbing, and kayaking.

In 2007, XYZ implemented a loyalty program that enabled it to collect data about its customers.

The data collected enabled XYZ to obtain invaluable insight about its customers and use that information to serve the customers better.

XYZ was, therefore, able to out-perform its rivals and grow at a fast pace. After 6 years, the company's growth began to slow down.

In 2013, the business stagnated. Rival companies caught up to XYZ using better analytic capabilities and these companies now have the same insight about the consumers.

In addition, XYZ is also facing increased competition from online retailers who are equipped with deeper insight about the clients because they have more far-reaching data on their online shoppers.

While XYZ's loyalty program has helped them, achieve greatness, it still accounts for roughly 20 percent of their total revenue.

They have restricted data about the remaining 80 percent of their customers. Online retailers, on the other hand, can create detailed profiles of 100 percent of their buyers, even on information such as which category of items a person is interested in, what does he/she view but not purchase, and many other details that are much easier to obtain if the store is virtual.

While conventional analytics has helped XYZ in the past, it can only go so far. XYZ now needs to take their clients' understanding to the next level. And this is where the big data and analytics come in.

So, why is big data analytics important for organizations?

Big data analytics can help organizations such as XYZ harness their data and use it to discover new opportunities.

This, in turn, can lead to smarter business moves, more efficient business operations, higher profits and happier clients.

In particular, big data analytics can help the organizations in the following ways:

- *Cost reduction*. Big data technologies like Hadoop and other cloud-based analytics bring significant cost advantages when it comes to storing vast amounts of data. In addition, this data can identify more efficient ways of doing business.

- **Quick and better decision-making**. With the speed of big data technologies coupled with the ability to analyze new sources of data, firms can analyze data immediately and make fact-based decisions that are based on what they've learned.

- **Development of new products and services.** With the ability to assess customer needs and satisfaction using big data analytics comes the power to give clients what they want. More and more companies are creating new products to meet customers' needs as a competitive strategy.

Where is Big Data being used in companies?

Few people will argue that firms have more data than ever at their disposal. But actually extracting meaningful insights from that data and even converting that knowledge into action is easier said than done.

Big Data Analytical Experts

Choosing a career is perhaps one of the most challenging decisions that you'll ever make. Not only does it affect your happiness but it also determines your how much money you'll be earning for the rest of your life.

Today, there are over six hundred careers in the world that you can choose from, making the task even more complicated.

If you are perceptive, curious, intuitive, inquisitive, and enjoy playing with numbers, then a Data Analytical job may be appropriate for you.

Besides, Data Analytical jobs are currently some of the highest paying jobs in the world. Here are some of the Big Data Analytical jobs:

#1: Data Management Professional

A Data Management Professional is essentially an IT role, akin to the role played by a Database Administrator.

The Data Management Professional is concerned with handling data and the infrastructure that supports it.

There is little to no data analysis in this role. A knowledge of application of languages such as Python and R even though is a plus, but not necessary.

SQL can help, as well as Hadoop and other related query languages such as Hive or Pig.

The key technologies and skills that Data Management Professional focuses on include:

- Apache Hadoop and its ecosystem
- Apache Spark and its ecosystem
- RDBMSs
- NoSQL databases

#2: Data Engineer

A Data Engineer is a big data and non-analytic career path. The key roles of a Data Engineer involve designing and implementing the database infrastructure.

If the data management professional were the car mechanic, then data engineering would be the automotive engineer.

But don't confuse the two roles. Both of these big data roles are essential to both the delivery and continued functioning of the database and are of equal importance when implemented.

As a matter of fact, the technologies and skills required for data engineering and data management are similar.

Although the extent of your can understanding for these concepts may vary.

#3: Business Analyst

A Business Analyst's roles is strictly analyzing and presenting the data. This role includes activities such as reporting, dashboards, and anything referred to as "Business Intelligence."

This position often requires interaction with—or querying of—databases, both the relational and non-relational databases such as big data.

While Database Management Professional and Data Engineer roles were related to designing the infrastructure that manages the data as well as the actual management of data, Business Analysts are primarily concerned with pulling insight from the data, more or less as it currently exists.

Because of this, Business Analysts must have a unique set of skills that include:

- RDBMSs
- NoSQL databases
- Commercial reporting and the dashboard package know-how
- Data warehousing

#4: Machine Learning Researcher/Practitioner

Machine learning researchers and professionals are these large data professionals that craft and use the predictive and other correlative tools to leverage big data.

Machine learning algorithms apply statistical analysis at high speeds, and those professionals who wield these algorithms are not always content with letting the data speak for itself in the current format.

Interrogating big data is the modus operandi of any machine learning system. However, with enough statistical understanding Machine Learning Researchers can unearth hidden insight in data.

The key technologies and skills that Machine Learning Researchers focuses on include:

- Statistics
- Algebra and calculus (intermediate level for the practitioners and advanced level for researchers)
- Programming skills such Python, C++, or other general-purpose programming languages
- Learning theory (intermediate level for the professionals and advanced level for scientists)

#5: Data Scientist

The Data Scientist professional is concerned primarily with the big data and any of the stories it can provide, regardless of what technologies or tools have been used to carry out that task.

The Data Scientist can use any of the technologies, depending on their exact role to discover hidden insights to a significant set of data.

The key techniques and skills that Data Scientists focus on are:

- Statistics
- Programming languages such as Python, R, SQL
- Data visualization skills
- Communication skills

Challenges of Big Data

Big data is the new realism of the digital economy, presenting a virgin territory for organizations to take advantage and generate new value.

In other words, the big data prospects appear to be endless. But beneath these opportunities, lie some challenges that organizations must overcome to benefit from big data fully.

Here are some big data challenges that firms are currently facing:

a) Data quality

To begin with the big data adventure, you must first identify and regularly "clean up" the data that you want to work with.

Given the immense volume and the variety of data that is available, the quality of the data you use has to be given priority.

Conventional databases contain all sorts of errors (most of them are often human errors) that should be corrected for the requisite database standards to be met.

On that basis, a data quality audit should be your first undertaking in any big data system. However, the process of cleaning up the data to ensure quality is maintained is laborious and tedious.

b) Processing data

Data is everywhere and is never presented in the same manner. Each database has its own format.

For some database experts, the main issue in big data is more about processing than about the volume.

Automated data management and manipulation systems have become indispensable to advance the intelligence of the data, just like analyzing the data in real time.

c) Data protection

The majority of data collected by organizations for strategic purposes are personal data that comes directly from the user accounts.

Using this data is therefore linked to the relationship of trust between the organization and its clients. Therefore, the security of this data is a decisive element for the future of big data.

The company should protect their client's personal data against any unauthorized or illegal processing including accidental loss, alteration, and destruction of the personal data by implementing the correct technical, physical, and organizational security measures.

d) The image of data

Today, a big data algorithm is no longer enough. To critically look big data head-on, its visual experience must be in tune with the hopes and limits of a variety of users—data scientists, marketers, or even HR professionals.

Visualization experts are currently facing challenges, both in the graphic rendering big data and in the development of techniques to access the information.

e) The humanity of data

The last, and perhaps the most unique challenge that companies face when making decisions about how to use their big data is how to respect the human beings behind the data.

The database user is not just a mere statistic. The purpose of the data should be to make the right connection with the user and to intelligently guide the company in the relationship between those who produce the data (customers) and those who use it (companies).

Chapter 3

The Ten Common Algorithms

A variety of data mining algorithms that helps to create valuable big data analytic platforms are available. For you to use a particular algorithm, you have to establish your goals that you would like to be achieved.

Various algorithms have been designed to deal specifically with some business problems.

Other algorithms have been developed to augment the current existing algorithms or to perform in new ways.

This chapter explores some of the common algorithms used in big data.

#1: C4.5

At its most basic level, the C4.5 algorithm constructs a classifier in the form of a decision tree. To do this, the C4.5 is given a set of data that represents things that have already been classified.

But what is classifier?

A classifier is simply a tool in data mining that picks a bunch of data representing things that you want to classify.

It tries to predict which class the new data will belong to. Here's how the C4.5 algorithm works.

Suppose you have a dataset which has a bunch of patients. You know various things about each patient such as age, pulse rate, blood pressure, VO2max, family history and so on.

In database terminologies, we'll call these attributes. Given the set of attributes, we may want to predict whether the patient will get cancer.

In particular, the patient can fall into any one of two classes:

- The patient can get cancer
- The patient can't get the cancer

Now, C4.5 is told the class for each patient. And here's how the C4.5 works.

Using a set of the patient attributes and the patient's corresponding class, the C4.5 algorithm constructs the decision tree that predicts the class for the new patients based on their characteristics.

The decision tree learning generates something akin to a flowchart that classifies the new data.

Using the same patient example, one specific path in the flowchart would be:

- The patient has a history of the cancer
- The patient is expressing a gene that is highly correlated with cancer patients
- The patient has tumors
- The patient's tumor size is greater than 5 centimeters

The bottom line in C4.5 is that at each point in the flowchart, there is a question about the value of a given attribute.

And depending on those values, the C4.5 gets classified.

C4.5 is a supervised learning since the training dataset will be labeled with classes where it doesn't learn on its own that the patient will get cancer or won't get cancer.

#2: K-Means

K-means generates k groups from a data set of objects so that the members of the group are more similar.

It is a popular cluster analysis technique for exploring the dataset.

Cluster analysis is the family of algorithms that are designed to form clusters in a manner that the cluster members are more similar versus the non-group members.

The clusters and the groups are synonymous in the world of cluster analysis.

Let me elaborate using an example.

Suppose we have a large dataset of patients. In the cluster analysis, these datasets will be called observations.

We know various attributes about each patient such as age, pulse rate, blood pressure, VO2max, and cholesterol levels.

In K-Means, we'll call this a vector representing the patient.

You can think of a vector as a list of numbers that we already know about the patient.

This list can also be interpreted as coordinates in a multi-dimensional space. For instance, the pulse rate can be one dimension, the blood pressure in another dimension and so forth.

So, how do we cluster together patients who have similar age, pulse rate, blood pressure and cholesterol levels?

We just enter the number of the clusters that we want, and the algorithm computes the values for us.

The algorithm selects points in the multi-dimensional space to represent each of the k clusters.

The clusters are also called centroids. Now, every patient will be closest to one of the k centroids.

Because they hopefully won't all be closest to the same one, so they will form a cluster around their nearest centroid.

We will now form the k clusters where each patient will be a member of a cluster.

Since the centroid will be in a different place now, the patients will now be closer to the other centroids.

In other words, they can easily change the cluster membership.

The key selling point of the K-means algorithm is its simplicity. Because it is simple to implement, it is generally faster and more efficient when compared to other algorithms, especially over large datasets.

However, the two fundamental weaknesses of the K-means algorithm are its sensitivity to the outliers and its sensitivity to the initial choice of the centroids.

#3: Naive Bayes Classifier Algorithm

It will be challenging to classify a web page, an email, a document, any other lengthy text notes using manual means.

This is where the Naïve Bayes Classifier algorithm comes in. As we had mentioned classifiers in the C4.5 algorithm, a classifier is any function that allocates the population's element value from any one of the available categories.

For instance, the spam-filtering program is a popular application of the Naive Bayes algorithm. In this case, the spam filter assigns a label such as "Spam" or "Not Spam" to all the emails the user receives.

The Naive Bayes Classifier is amongst the most popular learning method that is grouped by similarities. It builds machine learning models for disease prediction and document classification.

It can be used in the following instances:

- When you have a moderate or a large training dataset.
- If the database has several attributes.

#4: Decision Trees

Decision Trees provide excellent data analysis tools that can help you choose one alternative from several alternative options.

They provide a highly efficient structure that allows you to lay out options and examine the possible outcomes of selecting those options.

They provide you with a balanced picture of all the risks and rewards that are associated with each possible decision you settle on.

Decision trees are those types of supervised learning algorithms that are mostly applicable to classification problems.

These algorithms work for both the categorical and continuous random variables. At the outset, the algorithm starts by splitting the entire population into two or more similar data sets.

To split the population, the algorithm bases its logic on important attributes, which are independent variables that distinguish the variables.

Suppose we have a sample of 60 students that have three variables: Gender (Boy/ Girl), Class (IY/ Y), and Height (5 to 6 ft.).

Now 30 out of these 60 students play soccer during their leisure time. Imagine you want to create a model that can predict which student will play soccer during his/her leisure period.

In this problem, we need to split the students who play soccer in their leisure time based on highly valuable input among all the three variables.

This is where the decision tree will come in. It will split the students based on all values of the three variable and identify the variable that creates the best homogeneous sets of students.

The decision tree should identify the most significant variable, the value that provides the best homogeneous sets of the population.

#5: Neural Networks

Neural networks have different layers that can be used for analyzing and learning data. It is one of the most widely used algorithms for analyzing patterns.

Every hidden layer will attempt to detect patterns on the picture that is being learned. If the pattern is detected the next hidden layer will be activated.

That layer will again try to identify the model on the next picture.

Suppose you're dealing with the problem of recognizing the models of cars in your system.

Then basically, the system must be made to learn the different patterns such as the color, the number plate and various features of the car for the neural networks to learn and categorize.

Suppose you bring your first car for detection.

Apparently, the first layer of the system will detect the edges of the car. Then the following layers will combine other others that have been found in car data.

Ultimately, a specified layer will try to detect the wheel patterns or even the window profiles. Based on the number of layers in your car, the system may or may not be able to specify what is in the picture.

The more layers of the neural network there are, the more the system will learn the patterns.

The Neural Networks learn and attribute the weights to the connections that exist between the different neurons every time the network processes data. This implies that the next time it comes across such a picture, it will have learned that this particular image is likely associated with a particular model of a car.

Below are some benefits of the Neural Networks:

- They require less formal statistical training.
- They can identify all the possible interactions between the predictor variables and the target variables.

Some of the disadvantages of the Neural Networks are:

- They require high computational power.

- They may not provide accurate relationships between the target variables and the predictor variables.

#6: Support Vector Machine (SVM)

Support Vector Machine (SVM) learns a hyperplane and classifies the data into two classes. At the high level, the SVM performs a similar task such as C4.5 except that SVM doesn't use the decision trees at all.

A hyperplane is a function such as the equation for the straight line, y = mx + b. In fact, for a simple classification job with just two features, the hyperplane can be a straight line.

Let me use a simple example to illustrate the SVM. Suppose you have a bunch of red and blue balls on the table.

When the balls are not mixed together, you can easily use a stick to separate the balls without moving them.

When a new ball is added to the table, by knowing which side of the stick the ball has been added, you can foretell its color.

The balls represent the data points where the red and blue colors represent the two classes. The stick will represent the simplest hyperplane which is a straight line.

The SVM will figure out the function for the hyperplane. When the balls are mixed, the straight line may not work. When you quickly lift up your table throwing the balls in the air.

Lifting up the table is akin to mapping your data into higher dimensions.

In this instance, we move from the two-dimensional table surface to the three-dimensional balls in the air.

A ball on a table has a fixed location that we can now specify using the coordinates. For instance, a ball could be 20 centimeters from the left edge and 50 centimeters from the bottom edge.

Using the coordinate system, we can describe the system (x, y) as (20, 50).

If we had a patient dataset, each patient would be defined by various measurements such as pulse rates, cholesterol levels, blood pressure and so forth.

Each of these measurements will form a dimension where the margin is the distance between the hyperplane and any two closest data points from each of the respective class.

In the ball and the table example, the distance between the stick and the nearest red and blue ball will form the margin.

SVM tries to maximize the margin so that the hyperplane is just as far away from the red ball as the blue ball.

In this way, it decreases the chances of misclassification. SVM helps to map them into a higher dimension and then locates the hyperplane to separate the classes.

#7: Apriori

It uses association rules for databases that have a large number of transactions. I know you're wondering, "What is association rule learning?"

Association rule learning is an example of a data mining technique that learns correlations and relations among the variables in a database.

Let's say we have a dataset full of supermarket transactions. Imagine a database as a giant spreadsheet where each row in the spreadsheet is a customer transaction and every column represents a grocery item.

Consider the table that follows:

Transaction ID	Chips	Dip	Soda	Apples	Milk
1	X	X	X		
2	X	X			X
3	X		X		

By applying the Apriori algorithm, you can learn the grocery items that have been purchased together using the association rules.

For instance, you can find out those items that tend to be bought together more frequently than others with the primary goal of getting your shoppers to buy more. Together, these items will be called item sets.

For instance, you can probably see that chips and dip and chips and soda seem to occur together frequently. These will form 2-itemsets. With a large dataset, it will be much more difficult to "identify the relationships especially when you're dealing with more than 3-itemsets. That's the where Apriori algorithm comes in.

For you to use the Apriori algorithm, three things must be defined:

- Item set. Do you want to see the patterns for a 2-item set, 3-item set and so forth?
- The support. The support is the number of transactions contained item set divided by the number of transactions. An item set that meets the support is known as a frequent item set.
- Confidence level. The confidence level is the conditional probability of some item, provided you have certain other items in the item set.

The basic Apriori algorithm is essentially a 3 step process:

- Joining. The whole database is scanned for how frequent the item sets are.

- Pruning. The itemsets that satisfy the support and the confidence transition to the next round for the 2-itemsets.
- Repeat. The process is repeated for each item set level until we reach the previously defined size.

#8: KNN

The KNN (k-Nearest Neighbors) algorithm is an algorithm that can help you understand and implement powerful tools of any supervised big data problem. The model for KNN algorithm requires the entire training dataset.

When the prediction is needed for the hidden data instances, the KNN algorithm will search through the entire training dataset for k-most similar examples.

The forecasting attribute of the most similar instances will then be summarized and returned as the prediction for the hidden case.

As we have seen above, the KNN algorithm belongs to the family of the instance-based and competitive learning algorithms.

It is an instance-based algorithm because the model uses the data instances or the rows to make precise predictive decisions.

We can also regard this model as an instance-based method since all the training data sets have to be retained in the model.

The model is also considered competitive learning in the sense that it internally uses competition between the model elements—the data instances—to make a predictive decision.

The overarching objective is to measure the similarities between data instances that provide the hidden data instance that is necessary for making predictions.

The model uses the lazy learning approach where it doesn't build its own model until the time that the prediction is required.

It only works on the model as a last resort to make predictions. Obviously, this has the benefit of only including the data that is relevant to the unseen data.

Suppose the problem at hand observes 150 variations of iris flowers from 3 different species. Out of these species, there are 4 measurements of the flowers that we're interested in. These are the sepal length, the sepal width, the petal length and the petal width.

All these measurements are in centimeters. Now we want to predict the hidden data such as the species of the flower whether it is setosa, versicolor or virginica.

For us to identify what species the flower is, we have to split the data into the training and test data sets. Once we have done this, we will now use the results of splitting to predict the Kth nearest neighbor.

In other words, we use the results that we have on hand to classify the flower based on its closest resemblances.

For instance, we can assume that good classification accuracy is above 90 percent being correct or 96 percent and predict the hidden data.

Here's the summary of how the classification will be done:

- Generate the input data. The input data forms part of the training data. In the flower example, we have 150 observations of the iris flowers from 3 different species that have different sepal lengths, sepal widths, petal lengths and the petal widths.

- Compute the distance between any two data instances (determine the Kth nearest neighbor) to determine the similarity levels.
- Locate the K most similar among the neighbors.
- Generate a response based on the data instances.
- Summarize the accuracy of the predictions.

#9: Clustering Algorithm

The clustering algorithm is an unsupervised algorithm that solves the clustering problem. Its procedure follows a simple way to classify any given data set using a particular number of clusters (assume that K clusters).

The data points inside a given cluster must be homogeneous and heterogeneous to the peer groups.

Can figure out the shapes from the inkblots?

Well, the clustering algorithm is akin to this activity.

In other words, you only look at the shape of the inkblot and decipher how many different clusters or population are present on that inkblot.

In particular, here's how the algorithm will allow you to solve the learning problem:

- The algorithm selects the K number of points for each of the clusters. For simplicity, these clusters will be called the centroids.
- Each data point formed will now create the cluster with the closest centroids. In this case, we will have K clusters.
- We now determine the centroid of each cluster based on the existing cluster members. This generates new centroids.
- Since new centroids have been generated, step two and three are repeated to find out the closest distance for each data member from the generated centroids. The process is repeated until convergence occurs.

As we have seen, we will have clusters, and each cluster will have its centroid.

The total of the squares of differences between the centroid and the data points within the cluster will constitute the sum of square value for that cluster.

Also, when the sum of the squared values for all the groups has been added, it will become total within the sum of square values for the cluster solution.

#10: Random Forest

If you're a data scientist, then I am certain you've used Random Forest algorithm in one way or another.

The Random Forest algorithm is considered to be the panacea for all the data science problems.

In fact, whenever you can't think of any machine-learning algorithm—irrespective of situation—always use the Random Forest but on a light note!

Random Forest is a versatile machine learning algorithm that is capable of performing both regression and classification tasks. It can also undertake the task of dimensional reduction methods, treating the missing values, the outlier values and other essential stages of data exploration.

It can be regarded as some sort of ensemble learning method that combines a group of weak models to produce a robust learning model.

In Random Forest algorithm, we grow the multiple trees as opposed to a single tree that we used in Decision Trees.

To classify any new object that has attributes, each tree in the forest provides a classification where all the trees determine a particular class. The determination process is similar to "voting."

The algorithm picks the classification that has the most votes over all the other trees that exist in the forest.

Here's how the algorithm works:

- Assume the number of cases in the training set is N. Then, the sample of these N cases is taken at random with replacement. This example forms the training set for growing the tree in the forest.
- If there are M input variables, then a number m<M will be specified so that at each of the nodes, m variables can be selected at random

from M. Now, the best split on m will be used to split the node where the value of m is held constant while the forest grows.

- Each tree grows to the largest degree possible without pruning.

Through aggregating the collection of the majority votes for classification and the average for regression of n-tree trees, we can perform a series of prediction of new data based on the predictive n-tree trees.

Chapter 4

NoSQL Technologies

The big data universe seems to have more than its fair share of languages, platforms and development frameworks. If you want to explore big data, you'll find that some alien technologies surround you.

Even though it may be difficult to understand the role of these techniques, some of them complement each other.

In this section, we explore the various database technologies and how they link with each other.

But first, we should define the NoSQL databases.

What is NoSQL?

NoSQL refers to those databases that don't follow the conventional tabular structure. In other words, data is not organized in the typical rows and columns structure as you are used to in the SQL databases.

An example of NoSQL is the text from social media platforms such as Facebook and Twitter, which can be analyzed to unearth trends and preferences. Another example of NoSQL is video data or sensor data.

Some NoSQL database technologies perform well for particular data problems. Examples of common NoSQL database systems are:

- Hbase
- CouchDB
- MongoDB
- Cassandra
- Hadoop

Let's jump in to explore these techniques.

#1: HBase

HBase is an open source, horizontally scalable and distributed column-oriented database system built on top of the Hadoop file system by Apache Group.

HBase has a data model that is similar to the Google's big table and is designed to provide quick random access to vast amounts of structured data.

HBase leverages its fault tolerance features provided by the Hadoop File System (HDFS) to create distributed column-oriented database.

Because of its Hadoop ecosystem, you'll have access to random and real-time read/write access to data in the HDFS.

You can also store the data in HDFS either directly or use the HBase. The data consumer can understand and access the data in HDFS randomly using the HBase system.

#2: CouchDB

CouchDB is an open source and NoSQL database system based on common standards that facilitate web accessibility and compatibility using a variety of devices. Specifically, the CouchDB is a document-oriented database system, and within each document, the fields are stored as key-value maps.

The fields can be either a simple key or value pairs, lists, or even maps. Each document, which is stored in the database system, is given a document-level unique identifier (_id) and revision (_rev) number for each of the changes that will be made and saved to the database.

CouchDB provides the following features:

- Easy replication of the database across the multiple server instances.
- Fast indexing and retrieval of data.
- REST-like interface for improved database operations such as document insertion, updates, retrieval, and deletion.
- JSON-based document format that is easily translatable across different programming environments.
- Multiple libraries for different programming environments.

#3: MongoDB

MongoDB is a leading open-source NoSQL database technology that is cross-platform compatible.

MongoDB has some impressive inbuilt features that make it an excellent choice for organizations that require fast and flexible access to their data.

Being a NoSQL database, MongoDB leaves out the relational database's table-based structure to adapt to the JSON-like documents that have dynamic database schemas which are often called BSON.

The use of BSON makes the process of data integration for certain types of apps faster and easier. MongoDB is developed for enhanced scalability, high availability and improved performance from a single server deployment system to large and complex multi-tier infrastructures.

Some of the MongoDB features include:

- Provision of ad hoc queries. MongoDB supports the search process by fields, regular expressions, and range queries.

- Enhanced indexing. Any field in the BSON MongoDB document can be indexed.
- High replication. MongoDB offers high availability through replica sets that have two or more copies of the original data.
- Load balancing. Sharding is the process that MongoDB uses to scale the database horizontally. This means that the data will be distributed and split into multiple ranges and then stored in different shards that can be located on different servers. In this case, the shard keys are used to find out how the data will be distributed.
- Aggregation. When used with MapReduce, MongoDB can enable batch processing of data as well as perform complex aggregation operations.

#4: Cassandra

Cassandra is an open source and distributed storage system (database) that is used to manage vast amounts of database spread out across the world.

It provides a highly available service that has no single point of failure.

Essentially, Casandra is a scalable, consistent and fault tolerant NoSQL database system that uses column-oriented design to create a database that mirrors the Google Bigtable.

Casandra was developed at Facebook and implements a Dynamo-style replication model that is fault tolerant with the addition of a robust column family data model. Casandra has the following features:

- Elastic scalability. Cassandra is a highly scalable system. It allows the addition of more hardware to accommodate more clients and more data as per the user requirements.
- Always-on architecture. Cassandra has no single point of failure. This means that it is always available for business-critical applications that can't afford a failure.
- Fast linear-scale performance. Cassandra is a linearly scalable system. It increases the throughput as the number of nodes in the cluster increase to provide a quick response time.
- Flexible data storage. Cassandra accommodates all the possible data formats such as structured,

semi-structured, and unstructured formats. It can accommodate the changes to data structures according to user requirements.

- Easy data distribution. Cassandra offers the flexibility to decentralize data where the data is replicated across multiple data centers.
- Transaction support. Cassandra supports properties such as Atomicity, Consistency, Isolation, and Durability.
- Fast writes. Cassandra was designed to execute on the cheap commodity hardware. Therefore, it performs fast writes and can store vast amounts of data without sacrificing the read efficiency.

#5: Hadoop

Two computer scientists, Doug Cutting and Mike Cafarella, conceived Hadoop in 2006 to support the distribution of the Nutch search engine.

The development of Hadoop was inspired by the Google's MapReduce, which is a software framework where a complex task is broken down into numerous subtasks through divide and conquers approach.

The subtasks, also called blocks or fragments, can be executed on any node in a cluster.

The Hadoop technology makes it possible to execute the applications on systems with multiple hardware nodes and handle vast amounts of data.

Its distributed file system promotes rapid data transfer rates among the nodes and allows the technology to continue operating in case of node failures.

This method lowers the risk of disastrous system failure and unexpected data loss.

Since its initial launch, Hadoop has been regularly updated. The second iteration of the Hadoop (Hadoop 2) improved resource management and scheduling by featuring a high-availability filesystem option and support for the Microsoft Windows and other components that expand the framework's versatility for data analytics.

Hadoop also supports a broad range of related projects, which can complement and extend Hadoop's primary capabilities.

The complementary software packages are:

- Apache Flume. A system used to gather, aggregate and move huge amounts of streaming data into HDFS.
- Apache HBase. An open source and non-relational distributed database.
- Apache Hive. A data warehouse that facilitates data summarization, querying, and analysis.
- Cloudera Impala. A massively parallel processing database for Hadoop that was created by Cloudera, which is now an open source software.
- Apache Oozie. A server-based workflow scheduling system that manages Hadoop tasks.
- Apache Pig. A high-level platform that is creating programs which run on Hadoop.
- Apache Sqoop. A tool that transfers bulk data between Hadoop systems and structured data stores such as RDBMS's.

Apache Spark. A fast engine used for big data processing that is capable of streaming and supporting machine learning, SQL and graph processing.

Chapter 5

Big Data Technologies

To gain the strategic competitive advantage that big data holds, you must infuse analytics everywhere, make speed your differentiator, and exploit the true value in all types of data.

This demands an infrastructure that can handle and process the ever-exploding volumes of structured and unstructured data and protect the data privacy and security.

The big data technologies should support searching, development, governance and analytics services for all the data type such as transaction and application data, machine and sensor data, social, imaging and geospatial data.

This chapter focuses on some of the big data technologies that can help you take advantage of big data analytics.

At the outset, big data technologies can be summarized into the following:

- MapReduce
- Pig
- Hive

Let's dive in and explore these technologies.

#1: MapReduce

In 2004, two Google scientists, Sanjay Ghemawat and Jeffrey Dean, wrote a paper that provided a framework on how Google uses the "Divide and Conquer" approach to handle vast amounts of its databases.

The divide and conquer methods involves breaking a complex task into smaller sub-tasks and then working on the sub-tasks in parallel to generate results efficiently.

They referred to this approach as the MapReduce. MapReduce has formed the basis of some of the most popular and sophisticated big data technologies in the recent past.

Today, MapReduce is the cornerstone of Hadoop. MapReduce is a programming paradigm that allows massive scalability across multiple servers in a Hadoop cluster.

If you're familiar with the clustered scale-out data processing systems, then it is relatively straightforward to comprehend MapReduce.

MapReduce actually refers to the two separate and distinct tasks that the Hadoop programs perform.

The first task is the mapping job that takes a set of data and translates it into another set of data where the elements are split down into the tuples (key/value pairs).

The second task is the reduce job that takes the output from the map as input and combines the tuples into a smaller subset of the tuples.

Consider the following example.

Suppose you have 5 files where each file has 2 columns (a key and value in Hadoop terminologies) that represent the city and the corresponding temperature that has been recorded in that city for the various days.

You can imagine that the real application will be complex as it's likely to contain millions of rows where the rows may not be neatly formatted rows at all.

Either way, the city is the key while the temperature is the value. Suppose we have the following key/values:

```
Nairobi, 20
Singapore, 25
New York, 22
Johannesburg, 32
Nairobi, 4
Johannesburg, 33
New York, 18
```

Out of all the data we have gathered, we want to determine the maximum temperature for each of the cities across all of the data files (note that each of the records can have the same city represented several times).

Using the MapReduce algorithm, we can split this down into 5 map tasks, where each mapper performs on one of the 5 files while the mapper task works through the data to return the maximum temperature for each city.

For instance, the results generated from one mapper task for the above data will look like this:

```
(Nairobi, 20) (Singapore, 25) (New York,
22) (Johannesburg, 33)
```

Let's assume the other 4 mapper tasks (working on the other 4 files has not been shown here) generated the following intermediate results:

```
(Nairobi, 18) (Singapore, 27) (New York,
32)   (Johannesburg,  37)(Nairobi,  32)
(Singapore,  20)   (New   York,   33)
(Johannesburg,    38)(Nairobi,    22)
(Singapore, 19)   (New   York,   20)
(Johannesburg,    31)(Nairobi,    31)
(Singapore,  22)   (New   York,   19)
(Johannesburg, 30)
```

All the five of these output streams can be fed into the reduce tasks that combine data and output one value for each city generating the final result set as follows:

```
(Nairobi, 32) (Singapore, 27) (New York,
33) (Johannesburg, 38)
```

The results from each city can be reduced to a single count—the sum of all cities—to determine the overall population of the database.

This process of mapping people to cities in parallel and then joining the results (reducing) is much more efficient compared to sending a single individual to count every individual in the database in a serialized fashion.

#2: Pig

When Hadoop began to be implemented on a bigger scale, big data scientists soon realized that they were wasting too much time on writing the MapReduce queries rather than the actual process of analyzing the data.

The MapReduce code was long and time consuming to write. The developers at Yahoo soon launched the Pig as a solution to get around the problem of time consumption.

Pig primarily provides an easier way to write the MapReduce queries.

It is similar to Python and allows the development of shorter and more efficient codes that are written to be written and translated to MapReduce before the execution process.

#3: Hive

While the Apache Pig solved the problem of time consumption for some people, many still found the system difficult to learn.

SQL is a language that most database developers are familiar with and therefore developers at Facebook decided to create Hive as an alternative to Pig.

Apache Hive allows the code to be written in the Hive query language (HQL) which as the name suggests, is akin to SQL.

If you are familiar with Python, you can pick up the Pig to write code. And if you have knowledge of SQL you can go for the Hive. Either way, you get away from the time-consuming job of writing the MapReduce queries.

Chapter 6

Applications of Big Data

Today's big data analytics is used for the development of strategic, operational and tactical decision making across the industry verticals such as E-commerce, retail, banking, and sports.

Let us explore how big data can be applied in industries and businesses.

Retail

Big data analytics is used to provide the following insights:

- How to increase the profit margins at a product-level.
- Insights into customer profiles that can help answer basic queries such as who they are and why they make certain purchases using Market Basket analysis.
- Identify the items that are likely to be bought together.
- Which marketing strategies can work better than others?
- What is the optimal pricing?
- Personalized offers
- What is the efficient stock strategy?

Finance

The global financial big data analytics market is one of the fastest growing sectors of the big data industry.

Organizations can use big data analytics in the following ways:

- Shareholder metric analysis
- Working capital management
- Risk analysis
- Fraud detection and prevention

One good example is Experian, a credit reference agency that holds around 3600 terabytes of data containing people credit history from all over the world.

Won't the banks and financial institutions value these data and make use of them before they make an investment or loans?

E-commerce

E-commerce analytics can help firms convert data into insight, leading to better and more informed decision outcomes that result in optimal profits.

E-commerce firms can use big data analytics to understand:

- What is the acquisition process? How do visitors and customers find and arrive at the storefront?

- What is the shopping and purchasing behavior? How do users engage with the online storefront and which are products they frequently purchase?

- What is the economic performance of the system? How many products does the mean transaction have? What is the average order value and refunds that should be issued?

Sports

Sophisticated statistical models can be to analyze professional players' performance in sports such as soccer, basketball, and rugby.

A coach can use this insight to select good players who can win the game.

These days, sports analytics is a big business, and large corporations and clubs are using big data to gain a competitive advantage over rivals.

Here is how sports analytics is using big data:

- Better precision in the striking zones. In sports such as baseball, technology can be installed in all league stadiums to track the status of pitches during games.

- Data from wearable computing technologies is gaining interest in devices such as Google Glass and the fitness trackers that rely on big data analytics.
- Predictive insights into the fan preferences. Analytics can help advance the sports fans' experience as teams, and the ticket vendors compete with the at-home experience so that they understand their fans and cater to them.

Marketing

Understanding the customers and how to find more prospects is the key to sustainable competition. Big data analytics can not only help firms achieve this, but it can add value to other marketing potentials.

Here are some questions that big data can answer in marketing:

- How are our marketing ingenuities performing today?
- Which of the marketing strategies is viable in the long run?

- How can we enhance those marketing strategies that are not effective?
- How do our marketing initiatives compare with our rivals?
- Are our marketing resources well allocated?
- Are we using the right marketing channels?

Sales

Big data analytics can help identify, model, comprehend and even predict the sales trends and outcomes in a given firm.

- Big data analytics can help grow sales in an organization by:
- Determining what goods and services are selling and which ones are not selling.
- Determining the optimal inventory for the organization.
- Measuring the effectiveness of the sales force team and their optimal sales force size

Human Resource

Big data analytics can help HR managers by crafting a single view of all the relevant workforce and other HR related data.

These insights can help these managers make business decisions that drive business processes and enhance profitability.

Some of the key areas where data-driven analytics can be used include:

- Talent acquisition and retention
- Rate of attrition
- Optimization of the rewards and other benefits.

Social Media

Social media platforms are the forerunners in using Big Data to spur their business growth and creating a viable business model. One good example is Facebook. Facebook collects and process huge volumes of data from its 2 billion of monthly active users. These data are processed, analyze and are made available to businesses or individual for running their ad campaigns. (https://www.facebook.com/CollegeHumor/videos/10154972346327807/).

Harvesting and Leveraging on Big Data is what differentiates Facebook from Friendster and probably the very reason why Facebook survives and thrives into a successful company with market capitalization of approximate 490 billion dollars whereas Friendster stepped into history.

Many individuals, small businesses and large corporations are benefitting from the collation and analysis results of Facebook's Big Data in growing their businesses sales and branding awareness to their desired targeted customers.

Chapter 7

Big Data Whispers

Debating about the future of big data is beside the point because we are already there. Many market leaders such as Google, social media platforms and even governments are already using big data and advanced big data analytics in ways that seem futuristic to their chasing competitors.

Obviously, these companies have already defined their big data futures, however, as impressive as these programs may sound, they really only scratch the surface of what is possible in big data.

Let's dive in to explore how big data is being used in selected organizations.

Digital Footprints

Today, every business owners know that having a sound digital footprint is a pre-requisite to expanding their business. Among the leading companies using digital footprints are:

- Google
- Social media platforms
- Online storefronts

Let us explore how these organizations are using digital footprints

#1: Google

Is there a marketplace for my product? This is a common question that most firms usually ask. Suppose you were tasked to start a new health insurance brand in Singapore.

You may see the interest for health insurance sector for the last 5 years. Now, to contextualize the interest, you can compare it to the car insurance, life insurance, or even home insurance.

While health insurance interest may show a strong consistency; it doesn't always show signs of steady annual growth.

That is where the Google trends and keywords come in.

To get a better understanding on the exact search volumes, you can use the Google Keyword tool and Google Trend to check how many searches have been made in a month for "health insurance" in Singapore.

You may find that the visual health insurance doesn't appear to have the same search volumes as that of the car insurance in Singapore, but the cost per keyword click could be significantly less.

If you're looking for a lower cost, then you could make the case that the cost per every client sign up may work out considerably less than the car insurance.

#2: Online storefronts

Here is how big data and advanced analytics is helping online storefronts such as Amazon, eBay, and Alibaba to increase sales:

- Personalization of the items. Data from several touch points is processed in real-time to provide the shopper a personalized experience such as content and promotions.

- Dynamic pricing. Online storefronts must have dynamic pricing if their products are to compete on price with other firms. This demands data from multiple sources like the competitor pricing, product sales, and customer actions to determine the appropriate price to close the sale.

- Customer service. Excellent customer service is crucial to the success of online storefronts. To continue excelling at customer service, online retailers should use big data and advanced analytics to understand their customers better.

#2: The U.S Government

The following are instances where the federal agencies and non-federal organizations are applying big data and advanced analytics:

a) Fraud detection

The Social Security Administration (SSA) is using the big data and advanced analytics to analyze vast amounts of unstructured data that appear in the form of disability claims.

The SSA can now process medical taxonomies, and other expected diagnosed more rapidly and efficiently make informed choices without fraudulent claims.

b) Health-Related Research

The Food and Drug Administration (FDA) is using big data and advanced analytics across its many labs involved in testing to study the patterns of foodborne illness. The database which is part of the agency's Technology Transfer program enables the FDA to respond more promptly to the contaminated products that enter the food supply chain and contribute to over

325000 hospitalizations and 3000 deaths that are related to foodborne illness every year.

c)   Government Oversight and Education

The U. S. Department of Education is applying data mining and advanced machine learning analytics to enhance teaching and learning.

The advanced analytics can detect boredom from the patterns of key clicks and redirect the student's attention.

Since this data is collected in real-time, there is a real chance of continuous improvement through multiple feedback loops that operate seamlessly at different time scales.

CONCLUSION

We are living in a data loaded and data-driven world. Today, data has transformed companies in ways we never imagined decades ago. So much big data of what we do is either being recorded or stored somewhere. Firms both big and small, traditional and non-traditional are using big data to understand their customers better.

As a matter of fact, big data helps these firms to target the appropriate customers and improve their purchasing experiences. The insights gained from analyzing big data helps businesses to identify new growth areas and product opportunities, streamline their costs, increase their operating margins and above all, make better human resource decisions and more efficient budgets.

The future, as many say belongs to only those who embrace big data. Now you have taken that right first step. By reading this book, we hope that you can gain valuable experiences on how big data is revolutionizing organizations. We now trust that you get started at acquiring those skills you need to join the big data revolution. All the best!

FURTHER RESOURCES

Below is a list of websites for useful Big Data resources:

a) https://www.planet-data.eu
b) https://www.sics.se/~amir/files/download/dic/introduction.pdf
c) http://www.dataminingblog.com/
d) http://blog.data-miners.com/
e) http://flowingdata.com/
f) http://abbottanalytics.blogspot.com/
g) http://www.kaushik.net/avinash/
h) http://blogs.webtrends.com/category/analytics/
i) http://statswithcats.wordpress.com/
j) http://www.bzst.com/
k) www.analyticstraining.com
l) http://support.sas.com/publishing/index.html
m) http://support.sas.com/events/sasglobalforum/previous/online.html
n) http://www.thearling.com
o) www.kdnuggets.com
p) www.analyticbridge.com
q) http://analyticsindiamag.com
r) https://www.modernanalytics.com/wp-content/uploads/2014/07/Chapter-1.pdf
s) http://www.kaggle.com/

t) https://www.cs.duke.edu/courses/spring13/compsci590. 2/slides/compsci590.02_spring13_lec1.pdf

u) http://www.oracle.com/technetwork/database/bigdata-appliance/overview/bigdatasql-datasheet-2934203.pdf

v) https://www.homeworkmarket.com/sites/default/files/q x/15/10/20/09/tutorial__big_data_analytics__concepts_t echnologies_and_applica1.pdf

w) https://woocommerce.com/2015/05/big-data-starter-guide/

x) LinkedIn Groups such as:

- SAS analytics and BI
- Business analytics
- Advanced analytics
- Data Science Central
- India analytics network
- Global analytics network
- Kdnuggets analytics and data mining

NOTES

Chapter 1

a) https://www.planet-data.eu/sites/default/files/presentations/Big_Data_Tutorial_part4.pdf

b) https://www.sics.se/~amir/files/download/dic/introduction.pdf

c) https://www.modernanalytics.com/wp-content/uploads/2014/07/Chapter-1.pdf

Chapter 2

a) https://www.sics.se/~amir/files/download/dic/introduction.pdf

b) https://www.modernanalytics.com/wp-content/uploads/2014/07/Chapter-1.pdf

c) https://www.snia.org/sites/default/education/tutorials/2012/fall/big_data/RobPeglar_Introduction_to_Analytics_Big_Data_Hadoop.pdf

Chapter 3

a) https://www.cs.duke.edu/courses/spring13/compsci590.2/slides/compsci590.02_spring13_lec1.pdf

b) www.kdnuggets.com

Chapter 4

a) https://www.planet-data.eu/sites/default/files/presentations/Big_Data_Tutorial_part4.pdf

b) http://www.ccs.neu.edu/home/kathleen/classes/cs3200/20-NoSQLMongoDB.pdf

c) http://www.oracle.com/technetwork/database/bigdata-appliance/overview/bigdatasql-datasheet-2934203.pdf

Chapter 5

a) http://www.oracle.com/technetwork/database/bigdata-appliance/overview/bigdatasql-datasheet-2934203.pdf

b) https://www.homeworkmarket.com/sites/default/files/qx/15/10/20/09/tutorial__big_data_analytics__concepts_technologies_and_applica1.pdf

c) https://www2.wwt.com/wp-content/uploads/2015/03/Brief-Emerging-Big-Data-Technologies.pdf

Chapter 6

a) www.analyticstraining.com

b) http://support.sas.com/publishing/index.html

c) https://www.facebook.com/CollegeHumor/videos/10154972346327807/

d) https://www.forbes.com/sites/bernardmarr/2017/05/25/how-experian-is-using-big-data-and-machine-learning-to-cut-mortgage-application-times-to-a-few-days/4/#4afd9666513d

Chapter 7

a) https://woocommerce.com/2015/05/big-data-starter-guide/

b) http://analyticsindiamag.com

ABOUT THE AUTHOR

Victor Finch is a zealous enthusiast for the latest technology, innovative gadgets and financial subjects ranging from Fintech to stock trading. These interests strike a deep resonating chord in his passions. He is an entrepreneur, an IT consultant, and a part-time author.

Victor as a child was always fascinated with how things worked; breaking apart his childhood toys is a common sight. Victor always has some innovative workarounds or solutions for his friends or family's problems such as a stubborn laptop that just like to "sleep" and how to improve the quality of life for his family.

If you spot someone, penning down his thoughts while walking down the streets of New York. That could be our dear Victor. He is always intrigued by the latest creativities around and just wants to tinkle with them when he has some me time.

In his spare time, Victor likes to explore the world, read his favorite books, open his little notes and write his next best selling book.

Victor's Message

Thank you for purchasing and reading my book on Big Data! I hope you have acquire a reasonable and basic understanding of Big Data and how can applies to your business with various examples shared in this book. You may like to consider the prequel to this book, *Data Analytics for Beginners*, to further your knowledge and understanding on the topic.

If you would like to read more great books like this one, why not subscribe to our website.

https://www.auvapress.com/vip

Thanks for reading!
Please add your short review on Amazon
and let me know what your thoughts! – Victor

Other Victor's Titles You Will Find Useful

Blockchain Technology

Blockchain is a revolution that you should not ignore anymore.
Imagine you are been presented with an opportunity before the flourishing of Internet, what would you do? Now is the time!

THE ESSENTIAL QUICK & EASY BLUEPRINT TO UNDERSTAND BLOCKCHAIN TECHNOLOGY AND CONQUER THE NEXT THRIVING ECONOMY! GET YOUR FIRST MOVER ADVANTAGE NOW!

—— VICTOR FINCH ——

https://www.amazon.com/dp/B01N1X3C75/

- You will understand everything you need to know about the mechanics of Blockchain.
- You will learn how you can benefit from Blockchain
- You will learn the legal implications of Blockchain technology

Victor Finch

ISBN: 978-1-5413-6684-8   Paperback: 102 Pages

eBook, Audiobook Available

Are you still wondering or clueless about what is Bitcoin? Do you know Bitcoin is thriving robustly as a digital currency because of its characteristics for more than 8 years.

https://www.amazon.com/dp/B06XF6JK96/

- You will understand everything (including merits & demerits) you need to know about Bitcoin
- You will learn how to use Bitcoin and read the transactions.
- You will learn discover the best practices in using Bitcoin securely.

Victor Finch

ISBN: 978-1-5441-4139-8   Paperback: 98 Pages

eBook, Audiobook Available

Smart Contracts

Smart Contract is about the revolutionary (Blockchain Technology) approach with legal contracts or any legal agreements. This book offers an unprecedented peek into what the future may be like that could possibly change and enhance the traditional way of doing things for the better (many benefits).

https://www.amazon.com/dp/B06XW4L48F/

- You will learn how disruptive (positive) are Smart Contracts
- You will learn about the legal perspectives of Smart Contracts.
- **BONUS Highlight:** More than 7 Possible Smart Contract Use Cases in different industries.

Victor Finch
ISBN: 978-1-5446-9150-3   Paperback: 106 Pages
eBook, Audiobook Available

Data Analytics For Beginners

Leading companies must not only compete on faster ROI within the shortest time but also face stiff competition in this challenging digital frontier. Time is precious and marketing effort is worthless without information knowledge and precision execution. Data Analytics is your answer

https://www.amazon.com/dp/B071FM45GV/

- You will be expose to the big picture of Business Intelligence Data Analytics and its competitive advantages
- You will what is data mining in details and how can it work for you
- You will have a practical introduction on the four important steps in Data Analytics and explore the data analytics patterns

Victor Finch
ISBN: 978-1-5466-4191-9   Paperback: 127 Pages
eBook, Audiobook Available

Other Titles You Will Find Useful

Python

Python is a highly sought after skillset by many corporations. Possibilities with Python are limitless and often prefer over Java and C++ due to three characteristics that you will discover in this book.

https://www.amazon.com/dp/B06W2KKJK3/

- You will learn how to set up your first python.
- You will learn how to properly do error handling and debug to save you hours of time.
- BONUSES Included (plus Hands On Challenges)

Ronald Olsen

ISBN: 978-1-5426-6789-0   Paperback: 152 Pages

eBook, Audiobook Available

Python (Advanced)

Python (Advanced) is written for programmers, web developers, enterprise software engineers who seek to improve and enhance their programming skills with Python latest features, neat tricks that make your codes better, faster, lighter and more secure.

https://www.amazon.com/dp/B0732XKPSN/

- You will learn all about iterators, generators, descriptors and many more.
- You will explore all the important features that Python offers for advanced programmers.
- You will understand and learn how to use Python's powerful data analysis libraries that are making Python bypass R.
- BONUSES Included (plus Fun Hands On Challenges)

Ronald Olsen

ISBN: 978-1-5481-5643-5   Paperback: 142 Pages
eBook, Audiobook Available

Machine Learning

Have you ever pause and wonder why some companies like Amazon knows what you like or browsing and make timely recommendations to you?

In this book, you will have a peek into what Machine Learning is all about and over the vast applications, which underpins this revolutionary AI technology.

https://www.amazon.com/dp/B072SF1Y1K/

- You will learn all about machine learning algorithms
- You will discover some of the applications that have been developed as a result of machine learning
- You will learn an important chapter that is fundamental to applying machine learning

Matt Gates

ISBN: 978-1-5470-3904-3   Paperback: 104 Pages

eBook, Audiobook Available

Raspberry Pi

Raspberry Pi is a power minicomputer that has versatile uses and applications as such DIY security camera etc. The fun and innovative possibilities with Raspberry Pi is almost limitless and up to your imagination, knowledge and skills. This guide is suitable for beginners with no prior technical knowledge or skills required.

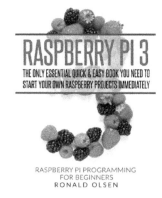

RASPBERRY PI PROGRAMMING
FOR BEGINNERS
RONALD OLSEN

https://www.amazon.com/dp/B06XG1N4K3/

- You will learn the in and outs of Raspberry Pi 3
- You will learn how to set up Raspberry Pi 3.
- You will discover some of the fun, interesting and useful Raspberry projects

Ronald Olsen
ISBN: 978-1-5441-4145-9   Paperback: 102 Pages
eBook, Audiobook Available

AUVA PRESS

AUVA Press commits lots of effort in the content research, planning and production of quality books. Every book is created with you in mind and you will receive the best possible valuable information in clarity and accomplish your goals.

If you like what you have seen and benefited from this helpful book, we would appreciate your honest review on Amazon or on your favorite social media.

Your review is appreciated and will go a long way to motivate us in producing more quality books for your reading pleasure and needs.

Visit Us Online

AUVA PRESS Books
https://www.auvapress.com/books

Register for Updates
https://www.auvapress.com/vip

Contact Us

AUVA Press books may be purchased in bulk for corporate, academic, gifts or promotional use.

For information on translation, licenses, media requests, please visit our contact page.
https://www.auvapress.com/contact

- END -